Cooking with Beer

Season by Season

Ken Birch

Published by Ken Birch

Publishing partner: Paragon Publishing, Rothersthorpe

First published 2006

© Ken Birch 2006

ISBN 1-899820-20-5 Paperback

Book design, layout and production management by Into Print

www.intoprint.net

Printed and bound in UK and USA by Lightning Source

Contents

Dedications

Many thanks to all of the following, whose help and generous support made this book possible:

Paul Hutchings and John Clarke of *Opening Times* for allowing the reproduction of original recipes.

Shirley La Pierre and Jim Loughran – photography.

Mike Ryan – typing, transposition.

Rosalynne and Liam Birch – typing, digification.

Mark Webb – design, typesetting and a great deal of advice and help.

Foreword (is four armed!)

Kooking with Ken Birch

"I'll never forget the first time I met Ken Birch – His TV series 'Jazz' had just been aired on BBC2 and I had a few questions for him about the colour of sock that Charlie Parker was wearing when he recorded... sorry... Ken who? Oh, Birch.

I'll never forget the first time I met Ken Birch – He'd just returned from an expedition around the bar and was carrying a handful of trophies that he'd collected on his travels. There were several pint pots, one ashtray and a handful of other native trinkets; beer mats, nuts etc.

We set up camp at a convenient table and watched in wonder at the comings and goings, the hustle and bustle of what Ken, the intrepid traveller called 'the regulars'. In time, Ken taught me the techniques of blending in with 'the regulars' at a variety of tribal watering holes – The Dock and Pulpit, The Crescent and The Kings Arms – until I too could pass myself off as a 'local'.

An important part of the nuances of cultural infiltration revolve around ritualistic activities such as drinking – no problem there – and eating. Now there's one thing about Ken – he knows his onions. Cooking comes as naturally to Ken as drinking, and when you combine the two the pleasure is... doubled!

Over the years, his column has brought many people a shiver of pleasure and a shudder of delight. It's called 'Ken's Kitchen' and has been a regular feature in 'Opening Times' for a pleasantly long time. Ken's culinary genius lies in his ability to blend combinations of different beers from a world of choices with food as varied as chicken, lentils, raspberries and wildebeest – alright, I made the last one up, but give him time!

Now collected together for the first time is favourites old and new from the gentleman chef himself, and it is in mouth-watering anticipation that I hand the rest of this book over to him."

C P Lee

Writer and Broadcaster

C P Lee is a Lecturer in Media Studies at Salford University. In addition to presenting and writing many radio documentaries on subjects as diverse (or maybe not so diverse) as 'Tiny Tim' and 'Jollywood' – The History of the Mancunian Film Corporation, he is well known as a 'Dylanologist', writing books such as 'Just Like the Night' – The Story of the Infamous 1966 Free Trade Hall Concert by our Bob; The Films of Bob Dylan and 'Shake, Rattle and Rain – A History of Popular Manchester Music from the 50's Onwards.

He is currently working on a history of the cult band 'Alberto Y Lost Trios Paranoias'. A band of which he was the Purple Heart – sorry, I meant Pulsing Heart. Like myself, he is currently a member of 'Colonel Lee's Mounted Ratigator's (NB), a band in somewhat of a hiatus ie, we ain't broken up – we just don't play!

NB   The Ratigator, a famous mountain man in 1830's America. He took his canoe down the Missouri and Mississippi rivers to New Orleans in 1841. His trapping skills soon enabled him to build a lucrative lifestyle catching and exterminating the rats which threatened to over run the city.

This story is entirely fabricated, but through many a telling, has gained a veneer of veracity.

KEN + C.F.LEE

Introduction

Let me begin by thanking you for buying this book, I hope you will not be disappointed, and I also hope to inspire some of you to experiment with, beer, cider and perry, to invent your own creations. I have laid down some techniques which I have found useful, but the artist in you may well discover new techniques. May the fates be with you!

Now, for a bit of personal history

In 1962, the week The Beatles first single 'Love Me Do', was released, I turned up for my first day at Liverpool College of Crafts and Catering, to learn all the fundamentals of cookery and catering. The huge injection of life that this wonderful city gave a 17 year old who had lived his last 3 years in rural, non-conformist North Wales is for another book, suffice it to say that the next 3 years saw Merseyside acclaimed as the as the centre of music, and youth culture in general:- an explosion of vibrancy, colour, creativity and vigour.

Upon leaving college with all my qualifications, I worked for sometime in Southport, Aberyswyth, South Wales and Manchester – sometimes cooking, sometimes in various management positions, but always using Liverpool as my base, and naturally picking up tips and recipes from the chefs/cooks that I worked with.

I had, by chance, gained a teaching qualification, (City and Guilds 142), and did a short stint teaching housewives at night school. I have often wished to do more teaching, but the Gods did not favour me, so the itch remains unscratched.

In 1967 while working at The Cabin Club in Liverpool, as Chef/Manager, I was found to have a very severe case of Pulmonary Tuberculosis, and returned to N. Wales to spend 7 months in hospital, and 18 months in staged recuperation.

Summer 1969 saw me back in Manchester, the place of my birth. I returned to catering, but having risen to managerial level, I found it hard to start at the bottom again, so I joined Hilti in September 1969. I must have liked the company, (which produces fixings and power tools to the building and allied trades), as I stayed for 23 years. In June 1992 a management (American) Putsch resulted in 40 plus of us older employees, booted out. Entering my evening local – The Marble Arch, Rochdale Road, Manchester, to drown my sorrows, I was offered two jobs, learning the ropes of running the pub on a part-time basis, whilst dividing my time as a sales rep for Phoenix Brewery.

This was my first experience of paid work involving beer:- wonderful, wonderful beer. But I had grown more aware of the world of ale through my involvement in C.A.M.R.A. Here is a brief history:-

<u>1971</u> Joined North Manchester branch of C.A.M.R.A.

<u>1976</u> Became Social Secretary – running various trips to Masham, the West Midlands and other places, over the following 5 years.

<u>1982</u> Attend my first G.B.B.F. (Leeds) – worked on membership and was obsessed by increasing number of members.

<u>1984</u> Became Regional Organiser, (by default), for Gtr. Manchester, and also joined Membership Working Party.

<u>1986</u> Appointed Chair of Students Liaison Group.

<u>1987</u> Resigned as Regional Organiser.

<u>1989</u> Appointed Andy Patterson (a student) to replace myself as S.L.G. Chair: also resigned M.W.P. having seen the membership rise from 16,000 to 32,000+

I had also worked with beer at several national, regional and local beer festivals, so I approached the trade not entirely green, (or so I thought).

After two months, I was deemed ready to run The Marble Arch full time, and so left Phoenix Brewery, having learnt something of how a small (ish) brewery operates; my thanks to Tony Allen and Sue Frampton, for their generosity, and help: the many differing ales smacked of quality then, and have maintained that high standard ever since.

Five enjoyable months, saw me head hunted to open a new conversion – The Crown, Heaton Lane, Stockport: part of Boddington Pub Co's small, real ale house division. Two very happy years saw the pub reach a good level of popularity, which, I'm pleased to say, has continued since I left in 1995.

After stints at The Gladstone, (now Bishop Blaize), Stockport and various times of emergency management at The Kings Arms, Bloom Street, Salford, I finally became Assistant Manager/Chef, at The Kings. It was during this period that I started experimenting with beer cookery; many of the dishes in this book saw their birth during those days.

Other beer related experiences followed, including being a partner in a micro-brewery, Bridgewater Ales, but that tale may be told at some other time.

Pre-amble

Before jumping in and rushing to try your hand at one of the dishes that follow, there are some important points I would like to make.

1. Like most recipe books, I intend the methods used as a guide only. So many things can vary, for instance, one tomato may be slightly smaller, slightly sweeter, have more seeds and less flesh than its neighbour, so precision is impossible. The golden rule is to stop and test as you go along.

2. Cookers and cooking vessels vary – a worn electric ring will not be as responsive as even a semi-blocked gas jet; pans can be thick or thin, shallow or deep. This will affect the amount of heat delivered to a dish. If too much heat is seen to be getting to the pan, take the pan off the heat, or move to one side. Turning the heat down will not have an immediate effect.

3. Make sure any bottled beers are de-gassed, by pouring into a glass and from there into another, until all the froth subsides.

4. Do not boil any dish with beer in; this will accentuate the hop bitterness, which is not a flavour most folk enjoy. Like all good rules, there is an exception – Ram Tam Yam Yam may be **gently** boiled to give a different flavour to the unboiled version.

5. Finally, try and use some of the techniques described to invent your own dishes, and don't be afraid of failure – eventually, you may create a classic!

Vegetarians please note

Vegetarian dishes are described on pages 17 to 40, also on pages 42, 48, 57, 61, 62 and 67-8.

Spring

Tripe with Cassis

Ingredients – for four people

4 tablespoons olive oil
2 finely chopped onions
1 teaspoon tomato puree
1¼ – 1½ lb beef tomatoes
2 lb cooked tripe
2 oz butter
4 oz grated parmesan
1x33cl bottle of Timmermans Cassis (or similar)
1 vegetable stock cube
Salt and black pepper

Method

Blanch the tomatoes in freshly boiled water for 30 seconds, turn over and leave in the water, off the heat until the skin starts to peel off (½ – 1 minute). Drain and cool under a cold tap – core and de-seed and chop into rough ½ inch squares, trying to retain as much of the juice as possible; then place on one side.

Cut the tripe into 1in wide by 6in long, strips and place in a bowl with the beer, heat the oil in a large saucepan, and the onions and sauté until golden brown. Drain the beer from the tripe and place on one side. Add the tomatoes, tomato puree and seasoning to the oil, and stir well. Stir in the tripe, butter and crumble stock cube. Simmer for 5 minutes, stirring constantly, reduce the heat and gently add the Cassis, beer – simmer very gently for 3 – 4 minutes.

Serving suggestion

Serve with grated parmesan on top.

Suggested beer accompaniment

Moretti, a Dunkel or ideally Forst Dark.

Kriek Smoked Ham Pie with Peche Beer Sauce

Ingredients (Pie) – for four people

3lb (approx) of smoked gammon
2 bayleaves
3 cloves + 2 teaspoons ground black pepper
2 sachets gelatine powder
1½ x 25cl bottles of Kriek (Cherry beer)
1½ – 2 sheets of frozen short crust pastry
(Sauce)
6oz plain flour
1 teaspoon clear honey
1 x 25cl BOTTLE Belgian Peach beer (Timmermans)
1 small onion
1 small tin of peaches
1 pint milk
salt and pepper
2 tablespoons olive oil

Method (Pie)

Cut the Ham (gammon) into 1inch cubes and GENTLY fry in a little oil with the bayleaves, pepper and cloves for about 3 minutes, turning frequently. Mix the gelatine according to the instructions and place in a large bowl. When cool(ish) add the Kriek beer and mix in well, then add the meat. Place in a large roasting dish or casserole and cook for 30 minutes in a medium (200 degrees) oven.

Roll out the pastry and when the meat is ready carefully cover the top of the roasting tray/casserole sealing the sides with a little eggwash (1 egg mixed with some milk) then return the oven to 230 degrees and bake for 25 minutes. Use the remaining eggwash to brush the pastry with, and return to the oven for another 10 minutes. Serve hot or cold.

Method (Sauce)

Gently heat the oil in a saucepan, finely dice the onions and sweat until golden. Slowly add the flour to make a golden roux then slowly combine the liquid thus: – a small measure of milk, stir in — a small measure of peach beer . stir in. Gradually increase the amounts of liquid, always ensuring a smooth sauce is evolving. About halfway through. remove from the heat and add the finely diced peaches, honey and seasoning. Return to the heat and carry on adding the liquids until the consistency of thin single cream is obtained.

Serving suggestion

Serve in a separate dish or sauce boat, with the pie.

Smoked Salmon Cider Bake

This is really an inexpensive dish. You can pick up 2lb of smoked salmon off-cuts for about £2 from a good fish stall. This should serve 4 people.

Ingredients

1 lb (457gm) smoked salmon trim
2 lb new potatoes
4 leeks
1 tablespoon mixed herbs

2 medium onions
1 pint cider
salt and pepper

Method

Roughly scrape the potatoes and slice into half inch (13mm) slices. Top and tail, peel and slice the onions into rings half inch wide: trim the leeks and cut into one-inch rings.

Break the smoked salmon into two groups – large chunks and flat pieces, breaking the chunks into thumb size pieces if necessary. Set aside along with the vegetables.

Gently heat (do not boil!) the cider, herbs and seasoning. Leave to one side. Take a pyrex or metal pie dish of sufficient size (10 inches x 4 inches minimum if round). Well you know these things come in round, rectangular, both deep or shallow and either short or long, so use your nuts! A foil dish would even suffice. Anyway, leave enough potatoes on one side for topping the final dish. Take the rest and blanch in boiling water for two minutes only.

Lay out the pie dish thus: a layer of leeks plus onions plus smoked salmon, then a layer of sliced potatoes. After each layer pour in some cider. finally topping with the sliced potatoes saved earlier. Bake in a medium oven (300C) for 25 minutes—test with a skewer to see when the potatoes are done.

Serving suggestion

For an added visual touch, the dish can be glazed by simply beating an egg with some milk about a 50:50 mix) and coating the top about 8 minutes before the end of cooking time.

Smoked Cod and Hapkin

This is a variant on a traditional Flemish recipe, but I tried it, many years ago in the centre of Belgium's hop growing area – Poperinge. Seafood and beer are particular favourites of Belgians and Hapkin is an especially fine, if subtle enhancer of any kind of fish.

Ingredients

4 cutlets of smoked Cod (or Whiting)
260g celery stalks – finely chopped
1 large bulb of fennel – finely chopped
2 tablespoons butter
2 tablespoons olive oil
1 tablespoon English mustard
20cl bottle Hapkin
15cl fish stock (or use a cube)
2 tablespoon coriander – finely chopped
Salt and pepper

Method

Season the cod, then heat the butter and oil in a large frying pan, add the cod and gently fry on both sides. Reduce the heat gradually and add the stock. Make sure the liquid is only gently simmering, then add the beer, simmer for ten minutes. Remove the fish and keep warm.

Add the mustard, celery and fennel to the liquid, stir in well and simmer for fifteen minutes. Return the cutlets to the sauce and sprinkle with coriander before serving.

Serving suggestion

Baked potatoes and green beans go well with this dish.

Suggested beer accompaniment

Swill down with a couple of chilled glasses of Hapkin.

Deep-fried Rags with St Sixtus

Another beer-influenced slant on a traditional dish. Remember to check out the suggested accompanying beers.

Ingredients

12 oz unbleached flour (with a pinch of salt)
2 large eggs, beaten
3 tablespoons olive oil
1-1½ litres of vegetable oil (for fying – quantity depends on siaze of pan)
4 oz caster sugar
3 oz icing sugar
1 25cl bottle of St Sixtus 12 or a very strong barley wine

Method

1. In a large mixing blowl, blend the flour, eggs, olive oil, salt and half the beer by this method. Make a well in the centre of the flour, add the eggs and fold flour from the edges over the eggs. Repeat this until all the liquids have been added.

2. Turn the dough out onto a large wooden or plastic board and knead vigorously for 20 minutes. Get your breath back, then return the dough to the mixing bowl, cover it with a warm damp cloth, sit down, have a fag and drink the rest of the beer – you've earned it!

3. After an hour, turn the dough onto the board and roll out until about 2 inches thick and then cut it into strips, 1½ by 4 inches.

4. Heat the vegetable oil in a deep fryer and fry your strips until golden brown – about one minute. Try and fry them individually but in any event don't try to fry more than three pieces at any one time. Remove from the oil, drain on kitchen paper, sprinkle with icing sugar and serve.

Suggested beer accompaniment

Try a peche, belgian wheat beer or perhaps an American-style ale such as Roosters Special, Bazens' Flatbac or Phoenix Arizona.

Belgian Sea Pie

Ingredients (for 4)

4 fillets of Whiting or Haddock
12 Mussels (shelled)
½ pint Brown Shrimps (Morecambe Bay Shrimps)
¼ lb rough cut Smoked Salmon
½ pint fish stock
½ La Chouffe
1 glass medium dry white wine
½ pint milk
4 tsp Fennel seeds
Salt and black pepper
1 lb mashed potatoes

5-6 cloves of garlic
4oz plain flour
2 tbsp vegetable oil
A little Cayenne or Paprika
1 large onion (finely chopped)

Method

Peel, cook and mash the potatoes (or boil the kettle and mix the instant!)

Cut the fish into ½ inch slivers, then mince the garlic; keep all these bits close to hand (or leg!)

Heat the oil and add the sieved flour and salt until well blended, gently and slowly (the way they like it).

Add the milk then fish stock, to form a creamy, thick sauce. Remove from the heat and gently blend in the beer and all other ingredients, *except mash and cayenne*.

Turn out into an ovenproof dish (do a twirl and say Abracadabra), cover with mash and bake for 17 minutes and 23 seconds, or about 20 minutes, whichever appeals the most, at 225°C.

Serving suggestion

When nicely brown, sprinkle with Cayenne and serve...

Suggested beer accompaniment

...with La Chouffe?

Chilled Beer Soup

This recipe may come as a bit of a shock to some of you. It is a cold beer soup which may be served hot if my forecast of a warm, sunny spring proves somewhat less than foolproof. In this unlikely event, I recommend you to save the recipe until the halcyon days appear, but if a cold snap is blown in by some bellicose spirit, then you may feel justified in serving this warm.

Before I list the ingredients, I have devised an easy method of measuring using a pint glass (for 6-8 portions) or a half-pint (3-4 portions). I am using the half-pint in this instance – just double up for twice the amount of soup.

Ingredients

6 oz of either green split lentils, red lentils, split green peas or a mixture of all three.
3 cloves of garlic
6 basil leaves
3 limes or 2 dessert spoons of lime juice
½ pint light ale or a light coloured bitter
½ pint cider
4 wheat crackers
2 oz cheddar
salt and pepper (to taste)

Method

1. De-gas beer and cider, if necessary, and place on one side.

2. Place the lentils and basil leaves in a half-pint glass.

3. Crush and finely chop the garlic into 1 teaspoon of salt – then add to the glass.

4. Add the lime juice – then top up with cold water.

5. Place the contents of the glass in a 4-pint saucepan (or larger) and gently bring to the boil stirring constantly. Reduce to a simmer.

6. Add the beer and cider and again gently bring to almost to boiling. Reduce to a simmer for 25 minutes, stirring briskly 5-6 times.

7. Slice the cheese and place on crackers – grill until melted.

8. Cool the soup for 30 minutes and then chill for at least 1½ hours.

9. Spoon into bowls (with ice cubes if you like) and break the cheese covered crackers into thumbnail sized pieces to garnish. For the sceptical, I give you my guarantee that on a hot spring or summer day, nothing is as satisfying.

If your local shops don't stock the beers mentioned in the recipes, check out the beer supplier list at the end of the book.

Beer Mushroom Risotto

Ingredients

1 bottle Sierra Nevada ale
4-5 fresh brown mushrooms
¼ oz. dried porcini mushrooms
1 medium onion, finely chopped
1 ½ cups arborio. or short grain, rice
3/4 pint made up vegetable or beef stock
teaspoon chopped thyme
6 finely chopped sun-dried tomatoes
2 cloves finely chopped garlic
2 oz. butter
4 fl.oz. olive oil
4 oz. grated parmesan

3 tablespoons chopped parsley
salt and pepper

Method

De-gas the beer and heat in saucepan until just below boiling point. Remove from heat and add the mushrooms. Soak for 20 minutes and drain the liquid, which you need to keep for future use. Rinse the brown mushrooms and chop coarsely. Keep the rehydrated porcini mushrooms separate.

Take a four or six-pint saucepan, add the mushroom soaking liquid. add the stock, bring to the boil and simmer for 23 minutes. Then place on one side.

In another, similar sized, pan, heat the butter and oil, add the onions and soften them for 5 minutes over a low heat. Add the prepared brown mushrooms and cook for a further minute. Add the rice and ensure that each grain has a covering of butter/oil. Stirring gently but constantly, cook until the rice turns translucent, then add the thyme and the re-constituted porcini mushrooms. Add one cup of reserved liquid and stir in on a medium heat until it has been absorbed. Continue to add the liquid at about half a cup at a time in this manner until it has all been used but remember make sure all the liquid is absorbed (just) before adding more.

Simmer for 15 minutes then test the rice – there should be a little hardness in the centre of the grain. Add dried tomatoes, garlic and seasoning and cook for 3 minutes, then add the parmesan. Stir this in and remove from the heat after 1 minute. The dish is now ready to serve with a hot dish or to cool, refrigerate for an hour and serve as a cold accompaniment.

Pollo Corleone
(not my name!)

(Italian Grilled Chicken)

This recipe is for two people. For more, use extra chicken(s).

Ingredients

1 small chicken
1 33cl bottle kriek
2-3 teaspoons olive oil
1 tablespoon dried oregano
2 cloves garlic
2 teaspoons coarse sea salt
1 teaspoon ground black pepper

Method

Make a cut completely through the underside of the chicken, then turn it over and score either side of the breastbone, until just scraping the bone. Turn the chicken over again and flatten it out on a hard surface; it may help to use the base of a heavy knife or cleaver. Score the flesh of the legs, thighs and breasts to a half inch depth, then rub the oil, pepper and half the salt well into the flesh.

Finely chop the garlic into the remaining salt. Pour the kriek into a basting dish large enough to hold the flattened out chicken and then add the garlic and oregano. Place the chicken in this and, again, rub the liquid well into the flesh (yeah! I'm well into the flesh).

Cover with clingfilm and refrigerate for at least 2 hours or overnight. Remove from the fridge and re-baste. Preheat a medium grill and place the chicken on the grill pan. As soon as it starts to brown, turn over and re-baste. Continue until both sides are golden brown and chicken is cooked through. Serve with a few slices of lemon.

Braised Pigeon in Goudenband

Ingredients (for 2)

2 Wood Pigeons
3 tbsp walnut oil
3-4 cloves of garlic
1 375ml bottle of Liefmans Goudenband
1 tsp dried rosemary or if fresh, use 50% more 1 tsp basil or if fresh, use 50% more
1 tsp English mustard (wet)   4 fl oz cider or tarragon vinegar
2 tbsp plain flour   Salt and pepper to taste

Method

Split the pigeons in two through the chest. Then, in a large saucepan gently heat the oil, rosemary, basil and garlic.

Remove from the heat and add the cider or tarragon vinegar.

Place the pigeons in a large casserole or roasting dish with the oil. Cook in a 220°F oven for 30 minutes. After 30 minutes add the de-gassed Goudenband and cook for a further 20 minutes.

Take a little of the braising fluid to one side. Take the flour, salt and pepper and sieve into a mixing bowl. Slowly blend the liquid in, to form a smooth, thick paste. Then add the mustard and let down the sauce with the rest of the cooking juice. If the colour is too light, crumble in an Oxo cube or two.

Serving suggestion

Coat the pigeons decorously and serve.

Suggested beer accompaniment

Wheat beers of varying ilk's could be a suitable swiller-downer, but really, you've bought a bottle of Goudenband to cook with. Why not buy another two or three to go with the meal?

Potatoes Hoegaarden

Ingredients (for 2)

1½ lbs Maris Piper or King Edward potatoes
1 red onion (2 if small)
1 white onion
2-3 cloves of garlic
½ pint Hoegaarden or Blanche de Bruges
4 oz flour
1 pint of milk
2-3 tsp dried parsley
2 tsp ground black pepper   A little salt
A little oil   (2-4 rashers of bacon may be added)

Method

Peel and slice the potatoes into ¼ inch pieces.

Peel and slice the onions by cutting in half, then ¼ inch slicing. Lay these to one side (or two sides, if you like!)

Form a roux with the milk, flour and oil. Remove from the heat and thin out with the de-gassed Hoegaarden. Place on the side (or sides). No, DON'T! Just remove from, or turn off the heat and leave it where it is.

Par-boil the spuds with some salt, i.e. bring to the boil and simmer 6 minutes 12.4 seconds, approximately! Cool in a sieve under cold, bright, sparkling, running water. Then, layer into a casserole dish thus – 1 layer potatoes, 1 layer onion etc.

Pour the thin sauce over and bake for roughly 20 minutes 18.2 seconds in a hot oven to 250°F.

Serving suggestion

Serve with a sprinkle of parsley.

Suggested beer accompaniment

Drink with a robust pale ale – Timmy Taylor's Landlord, say.

Summer

Welsh Rarebit

So you've done the rounds, had a few interesting beers and enjoyed good company. You feel at one with the world and well satisfied with life. You walk past the chippy a minute after it has closed, and suddenly an attack of the infamous munchies descends on you. What to do? Toast? Toast and jam? Or delicious Welsh rarebit? Of course the latter would water most mouths and provide a substantial weapon with which to attack the munchies.

My recipe will allow enough for 4 5 servings and which will keep for a fortnight or so – and provide a store to raid on those 'munchie' nights.

Ingredients

½ a small onion or 1 shallot
1 lb tasty Lancashire cheese
1 tablespoon flour
¼ pint milk
¼ pint pale ale
1 teaspoon dry mustard
A little oil

Method

Very finely dice the onion or shallot and sweat this in a little oil until soft. Gently blend in the flour and mustard, and stir until light brown. Slowly add the milk to form a sauce. Crumble in the cheese until ½ pound has been blended in. Then add some beer and stir, then some cheese and stir, and so on until each has gone. Leave to cool and place into a tightly covered plastic container. Refrigerate until needed. To serve, simply spread generously on toast and grill until slightly charred.

Grilled Prawn and Peach Salad

Ingredients – Marinade

1 tablespoon olive oil
2 tablespoons finely chopped shallots
½ tablespoon lime or lemon juice
1 lb peeled prawns
1 teaspoon Dijon mustard
1 teaspoon soy sauce
¼ pint Belgian peach beer
pinch of salt and pepper

Method

Combine all the ingredients (except the prawns) in a small saucepan. Bring to the boil, reduce the heat and simmer for three minutes. Cool to room temperature. Transfer to a bowl, add the prawns and refrigerate for at least 20 minutes. You can use fresh, uncooked prawns for this dish, in which case they should be placed under a medium grill for 3-4 minutes, turning three or four times. Threading them on wooden skewers may assist here.

Ingredients – Dressing

2 tablespoons olive oil
2 tablespoons finely chopped shallots
1 chopped clove of garlic
1 tablespoon sherry vinegar
salt and pepper
Blend all together with a whisk or fork – take about five minutes
Salad
1 cos lettuce
1 lollo rosso lettuce
1 ripe avocado
1 medium mango or peach
4 spring onions

Method

Chop lettuce into pieces about 2 inches round and place in a large salad bowl. Top and tail the spring onions, cut into rings and mix these into the lettuce. Carefully scoop out the avocado flesh (after removing the stone) trying to keep a half avocado in one piece: I could try and make this cleaner but just use your brains! Peel the mango or peach cut in half and slice into pieces about ¼ inch thick; repeat for the avocado. Leave these pieces on one side.

Toss the salad thoroughly with the dressing and lay the mango and avocado slices in alternate layers around the edge of the salad bowl. Remove the prawns from the fridge and roughly drain. Place these in the centre of the salad bowl and sprinkle with dressing.

Suggested beer accompaniment

Eat on the terrace with some well-chilled peach beer or a decent wheat beer and pray the sun stays out.

Read the beer notes at the end of this book to learn about the special qualities of the beers suggested as suitable accompaniments.

Kriek Kebabs

This tasty dish will serve 4

Ingredients

1lb lamb fillet (usually needs ordering from a good butcher) or 1½lb lamb chops
1-2 25cl bottles of Kriek (Timmermans, St Louis or Lindemans)
2 small redskin onions
2 cloves of garlic
2 teaspoons paprika

20 small (or 10 large) bay leaves
½ teaspoon salt
½ teaspoon ground black pepper

Method

1. Open the bottle(s) of kriek and de-gas by pouring into another jug or glass and allowing to stand for 15 minutes.

2. Dice the lamb into one-inch cubes.

3. Finely chop the garlic into the salt and add this, the paprika and black pepper to a bowl large enough to allow the lamb to be covered in liquid.

4. Add the lamb to the bowl. If you have some kriek left, save it. Cover the bowl and refrigerate for a least 4 hours or overnight. 5. Peel and halve the onions lengthwise and slice thickly (at least half-inch thickness). The bay leaves need to be roughly the same length as the onion slices.

6. Thread the lamb cubes, onions and bay leaves on to skewers, thus: onion, bay leaf, lamb, bay leaf, onion. lamb, and so on.

7. Preheat your grill to medium and cook the kebabs for 2 minutes then turn over (no. not you. – the kebabs) and repeat. Finally. turn the grill to high and finish each side, carefully watching for any blackening of the bay leaves, for 20 seconds.

8. Re-heat the risotto and lay the kebabs across it by running a fork along the skewer and gently removing the kebabs.

Suggested beer accompaniment

Kriek, of course, will accompany this dish perfectly, but a light red wine is a reasonable alternative.

Mixed Deep Fried Fish and Vegetables in Beer Batter

This dish needs to be prepared a few hours before any intended barbecue, but need not involve too much preparation. The quantities given serve four.

Ingredients (Batter)

4 oz plain flour (sieved)
1 large egg
¼ pint milk
½ pint pale ale
Pinch of dry mustard
Salt and pepper to taste

Method

Mix the flour with seasoning and the egg in a large mixing bowl. Slowly beat in half the milk using a fork or whisk. Repeat the process using half the beer. Keep slowly adding liquid in this manner until the consistency of thick wallpaper paste is achieved (don't worry, it tastes a lot better). Place in the fridge for ½ hour.

Ingredients (Fish and Vegetables)

The list is really up to individual taste, and can be all veggie, or include some fruit. Here is a suggested list.

4oz large shelled prawns
2 large smoked haddock fillets
2 medium trout fillets
1 cod steak
2 courgettes
1 parsnip
8 baby sweet corn
1 fennel bulb (very desirable)
4 shallots

Method

Cut the fish into 1½ inch pieces. Peel and top and tail all the vegetables and slice into pieces of the same size, except the fennel, which should be cut slightly smaller. Using a decent vegetable oil (corn oil or sesame oil), beat in a deep fryer to 350 degrees F. Dip the fish and veg into the batter and deep fry for 5 minutes, turning at least once. Drain onto kitchen paper.

Serving suggestion

Either serve immediately or keep in a sealed container in the fridge ready for use on that barbie.

The fritters are greatly enhanced by dipping into something saucy – try this one. Mix a large yoghurt with 3 teaspoons of crushed garlic, 2 teaspoons of tomato puree and a couple of pinches of cayenne pepper.

Chutney, Dips and Relishes

Several of the recipes which appear in this book can be enhanced by being served with one or two of the accompaniments I will lay out here. In addition, cold meats, fish dishes and several vegetable recipes can all benefit from the hint of beer. A bonus is that you may fancy a glass of wine with your food so a beery side dish may help assuage any guilt that you may feel at deserting the hop for the grape.

Rich Beer Chutney

This is suitable for cold meats or bacon butties. You will need 4 jam jars with a suitable seal.

4 medium onions
6 large tomatoes
2 red peppers
12 stoned dates
1 oz currants
2oz brown sugar
2 cloves of garlic
pinches of cinnamon, ginger, slat and black pepper
1 tablespoon vinegar (preferably sherry vinegar)
½ pint Delph Porter or old ale

Method

Scald tomatoes in boiling water for 1 minute; drain and cool. Then peel, core and finely chop the flesh.

Finely dice onions, peppers and dates. Peel and finely chop the garlic then crush into a little salt.

Gently heat enough oil to cover the bottom of a 4-pint saucepan. Sweat off the diced peppers (1 min.), then add the onions and garlic (2 mins.), finally add dates, currants and spices. Gently fry until all are soft. Add the tomatoes and stir in. Then add the sugar and the mixture should be briskly stirred until this has melted. Add the vinegar and the beer and simmer until a marmalade-like consistency is reached. Stand for 3/4 hour. If the mixture is too liquid, add the white of one egg and whisk on a gentle heat. Leave to set again. Pour into jam jars and seal.

Fennel Dip

This is suitable for fish. You will need.

1 medium fennel bulb
1 bottle Rodenbach
½ pint fromage frais
Pinches of ginger, salt and pepper

Method

Top and tail the fennel, keeping the bushy top for decoration. Dice into 1/8-inch squares and place into a microwaveable bowl with all the ingredients except the fromage frais. Microwave for 4½ minutes (750w) or 6 minutes (650w). Alternatively, place on the middle shelf of medium hot (gas mark 7) oven for 25 minutes. Strain into the fromage frais and gently fold in. Decorate with the fennel leaves.

Cheesy Rodenbach Dip

For use with crudites of dippy, crispy things. You will need:

½1b cheddar cheese, grated
½ pint garlic mayonnaise
1 bottle Rodenbach
Pinches of dry mustard, salt and pepper

Method

Very gently heat the Rodenbach in saucepan; add the grated cheese and seasoning. Stir until all the cheese has melted, then take off the heat and cool for 5 minutes. Spoon or fork the rnayonnaise into the beer/cheese combine, using the method by which a dollop is thoroughly stirred in before the next dollop is introduced. Cool and chill for ½ hour.

Chicks de Bourgogne

Another quick and simple dish which has the additional, sainted benefit of being cheap (if you consider the beer as mainly a luxurious accompaniment). It is also a veggie dish but can be carnified by the insertion of a grilled kebab.

Ingredients for two

1 can chick peas (curried or plain, as preferred)
1 small onion
1 tomato
2 crushed cloves of garlic
2 teaspoons dried ginger powder (or equiv)
1 dessert spoon methi leaves (optional)
1 teaspoon tomato puree
1 dessert spoon of Duchesse de Bourgogne (beer)
seasoning

Method

Finely chop the onion and sweat in a little oil for 1 to 1 ½ minutes – chop the tomato and add to the pan.

Drain the chick peas and add to the pan for 1 min. Stir in the tomato puree then add all ingredients except beer. When the dry ingredients have been blended in, remove the pan from the heat and gradually add in the beer.

My way of eating this meal is in a warmed pitta or nan, but I have also enjoyed it with cous-cous and I imagine it can equally well be served with rice or hominy (grits)

Suggested beer accompaniment

Drink with it the wonderful Duchesse de Bourgogne, which many specialist bars and off-licences stock.

Stuffed Mushrooms with Giradin

This tasty snack can be eaten chilled as a summer snack, or it can also be warmed to make an appetizing starter.

Ingredients (For 4 people)

4 field mushrooms
2 beef tomatoes
½lb feta cheese
1 large red onion
½ tsp oregano
¼ – ½ pint Giradin or other light Geuze

2 cloves of garlic
Black pepper and salt to taste

Method

Place the Mushrooms in a large baking tray or casserole dish and soak with a teaspoon of Geuze per mushroom.

Dice the tomatoes, or preferably make a concassé (See below). Peel and finely chop the onion, crumble the feta and add it to the mixing bowl. Crush the garlic together with the chopped spinach/rocket (some sprigs can be saved for decoration) and mix in with the seasoning.

Drain the mushrooms of the excess beer and fill the upturned base with the feta mixture. Cook in a medium oven, 220°F or medium grill, for 10-20 minutes. Serve immediately or chill if preferred.

Tomato Concassé

In a large pan boil enough water to cover the tomatoes; simmer for 5 – 10 minutes, then drain and run under cold water. Peel of the skin and de-core, finely chop, retaining as much juice as possible.

Suggested beer accompaniment

Serve with remaining Giradin.

Oriental Sweet Corn Fritters

Beer batter will usually improve most deep fried fritter dishes. This dish can be served hot or cold as a starter or snack.

Ingredients – for four people

1 medium can of sweet corn   2 cups + 1 cup of plain flour
½ pint of de-gassed light ale or bitter   ½ pint of milk
1 teaspoon of methi powder or 6 crushed methi leaves   3 cloves of garlic
½ teaspoon of chilli powder or 1 chopped chilli ½ teaspoon tumeric
1 teaspoon tomato puree   1 medium egg   Salt and pepper to taste

Method

Break the egg into a large mixing bowl and mix in 1 cup of flour, plus seasoning in. Add a little milk and then some more flour, some beer, some milk until two cups of flour have been taken in and a creamy batter has been achieved. It is possible that a little less beer and a little more milk is needed, so taste the batter, if it tastes too much like beer, add more milk: this needs to be done as you are going along.

Respectfully crush the garlic and all crushable ingredients and, together with the tomato puree, add to the bowl and mix in. Now wait! Cover and leave in a cool place for half an hour. Nip back from the pub and heat up a deep frying pan to 'not to hot'; whilst it is heating use the spare cup of flour to dust a suitable board. Roll some of the mixture out and form into round patties. Place into the pan, (about four at a time). Cook until golden brown – about five minutes a side.

Serving suggestion

Turn out and serve with a light chutney.

Suggested beer accompaniment

A lager, wheat beer or my favourite, a fruity mild, Bazens Black Pig would be a splendid washer downer.

Kriek Ice Cream

The idea of beer and ice cream may sound like inviting Osama Bin Laden to a barmitzva, but trust me the mixture works – believe me! Not only cherries and cherry beer but peaches and peach beer, raspberries and raspberry beer etc: I've even heard of Guiness so why not try it?

Ingredients (For Two)

1 330cl bottle of Lindemans Kriek (or any other not too sweet Kriek beer)
½ pint double cream
2-3 teaspoons icing sugar
10-12 cherries

Method

Pour the cream into a mixing bowl and whip, (does this term give emanation to the phrase 'lashings of cream'), until semi-stiff (no tittering boys). Gently fold in the icing sugar, then fold into it about 2-4 tablespoons of Kriek; taste as you add it to get the right amount of cherry flavour. Destone and halve the cherries and fold into the cream.

Freeze until set, making sure to churn the ice cream every half hour or so.

Suggested beer accompaniment

Use the remaining beer to accompany.

Autumn

Simple Beer Soup

This will serve four as a main course or eight as a starter

Ingredients

1 medium (400g) can chick peas
1 medium can red kidney beans
1 medium can cannelini beans
3-4 cloves garlic, chopped (or 3 squeezes garlic paste)
1 lemon
4oz Lancashire cheese
1 medium onion
A little cooking oil
1 pint bitter or any pale beer (de-gassed)
salt and pepper to taste

Method

1. Finely chop the onion and gently sweat in a little oil until golden.

2. Drain off the liquid from the canned peas and beans and set this aside. Add the peas and beans to the pan.

3. Stir in the chopped garlic or paste, salt and pepper.

4. Chop the lemon in half and add the juice of one half to the pan.

5. Now add ¼ pint of the beer and stir in over a gentle heat

6. Then add ¼ of the cheese, a further ¼ pint of beer and another ¼ of the cheese.

7. Either whizz everything up in blender, or mash with a potato masher or even a large fork and return to the heat.

8. Add further cheese to thicken and flavour and the juice from the other half of the lemon (tasting as you go). If the consistency is too thick, add more beer to thin. To thin further if required, slowly add some of the liquid from the cans.

I make these instructions about thinning because cooking pans vary enormously in the surface area offered to the heat; similarly cookers vary in the way they deliver heat to the pans. I hope I have covered all eventualities and that this will tempt you to try a quick, simple, yet different spring soup.

Suggested beer accompaniment

Since a thickish soup may cling to the ribs or, as I heard in Leigh once, "clack t't' xylophone bones", a refreshing wheat beer, or perhaps a good Czech lager may well wash it down a treat. My own choice would be a thin mild, let's say Hydes' Light.

Rodenbach Squash
with Fennel

Ingredients

1 butternut squash
1 white skin onion
1 bulb of fennel
salt
1 bottle Rodenbach
1 tablespoon dried fenugreek leaves (methi)
3 cloves garlic finely minced
1 teaspoon cayenne pepper salt
1 teaspoon lemon juice

Method

Cut the squash in half lengthways, de-core (take out the stringy bits in the middle), and then cut into two cross-wise, that is separate the neck from the bulb. Peel (this is hard work) with a sharp knife, and cut into half-inch slices. Place on one side. Top and tail the fennel, saving the green fluffy leaves for decoration, and cut into half-inch square pieces – well, as close as you can to half-inch square. Cook the fennel and squash in boiling, salted water (twice as much water as will cover the vegetables) for 8 minutes. Drain and cool under running water.

Top. tail, peel and slice the onion lengthways, then cut into quarter-inch slices. Place the Rodenbach in a large bowl then add all the other ingredients except the onion. Mix well but gently, then place the onion slices on top.

Refrigerate for at least two hours. To serve, carefully remove the onions, drain off any excess liquid and lay the mixture out on a bed of risotto. Decorate with the onions and fennel leaves.

Ham with Cherry Beer Sauce

Ingredients – serves 4

3oz butter
4oz finely chopped shallots
1 dozen stoned or tinned cherries
1 tablespoon lemon juice
2 tablespoons brown sugar
4oz vegetable stock (2 cubes crumbled into half a cup of hot water)
1 x 33cl bottle of Kriek
Pinch of ginger, pinch of Cayenne pepper
4oz flour
1 lb cooked ham or gammon steak (or 1 per person)

Method

Gently melt butter in saucepan, add shallots and sweat until soft. Then gradually stir in the flour and blend in, stirring, until it becomes a blond colour. Slowly stir in the lemon juice and stock and later the Kreik, until a smooth sauce is obtained; then add everything but the ham and adjust the sauce with a little milk or water if the consistency appears too thick. Simmer gently for 7 minutes and pour over the ham steaks.

To accompany this dish I have chosen a potato dish which can be used by vegetarians as a main course.

Pommes au Gratin et Biere

(potato with cheese and beer)

Ingredients Serves 4

6 large potatoes – peeled
1 pint Czech beer (Budvar for choice)
½ lb Gouda or Edam cheese
1 pint milk
1 tablespoon made English mustard
Salt and black pepper

Method

Slice the potatoes (about ½ inch thick) and layer in the bottom of a large casserole dish. Grate the cheese; *gently* warm half the beer in a saucepan and add the cheese to the beer, stirring until melted. Remove from stove, then add half the milk and the remaining beer to the casserole and season and bake in a preheated 400 degrees (Gas mark 8) oven for 20 minutes, turning the potatoes after 10 minutes. Turn the oven down to 200 degrees Fahrenheit (Gas mark 4). Return the cheese/beer saucepan to the stove and add the remaining milk and mustard – simmer for 2 minutes.

Pour the beer cheese mix over the potatoes and cook for another 5 minutes. Sprinkle with chopped parsely and serve.

Suggested beer accompaniment

To wash down both dishes why not try a light wheat beer or an American ale Frankiskeller or one of Roosters low strength brews – Ringo would fit the bill. Happy Gourmanding!

Somerset Sausages

Ingredients

This recipe serves four.

8 good class pork sausages (Porkinsons if you don't know a good butcher)
2 eating apples (Braeburns are ideal)
2 medium leeks
1 small onion or 2 shallots
1 tablespoon paprika
2 cloves of garlic
1 teaspoon tomato puree
½ pint of draught (real) cider or a bottle of Bulmers No.1
2 teaspoons cooking oil

Mis-En-Place

This term is used to describe the preparation of ingredients prior to cooking. For this dish preparation can be done while the sausages are cooking in a medium oven for 20 minutes (remember to turn them once).

1. Peel and core the apples, then slice into ¼ inch thick pieces.

2. Trim the leeks and slice into ¼ inch thick rings. Wash thoroughly.

3. Peel and crush the garlic; mince very finely into a couple of pinches of salt.

4. Finely chop the onions or shallots.

Method

1. When the sausages are cooked, remove from oven and place on one side.

2. Gently fry the onions for 1½ minutes; add the apples and stir for 2-3 minutes; add the leeks and, turning regularly, fry until they just start to brown.

3. Stir in the paprika, then add the tomato puree and garlic.

4. Add the cider slowly, blending all the time – an adjustment may be needed as the sauce should be thin but not watery.

5. Finally, turn the heat down until the sauce is barely simmering. Add the

sausages and warm through for 2 minutes. Be careful not to reboil as this causes congealing of the albumen in the sausagemeat, leading to toughness.

Suggested beer accompaniment

Cider would be a natural accompaniment, and of course would not disgrace this dish. But for the adventurous, why not try a bottle of Belgian gueze, or my own favourite, Liefman's Goudenband. Absolute Heaven!

Be adventurous and choose some exotic bottled beers to accompany your food.

Chicken in Perry

Ingredients

1 3lb roasting chicken
3 tablespoons olive oil
4-5 cloves garlic, crushed
1 pint dry or medium perry
1 teaspoon rosemary
1 teaspoon sage
4 fl oz red wine vinegar
2 tablespoons plain flour
salt and pepper to taste

Method

Divide the chicken into eight pieces. Heat a large saucepan with olive oil and add the garlic and herbs. Stir for about a minute, then add the chicken pieces, salt and pepper and cook until golden. Transfer to a flameproof casserole or oven dish. Cover with perry and add the vinegar. Cook in a medium oven (200-220 degrees, gas mark 6) for 45 minutes.

Remove the chicken from the casserole. Take a little of the liquid to one side and in a separate container blend with the flour to form a smooth paste. Stir this paste into the remaining liquid and simmer for 5 minutes.

Pass the liquid through a sieve. Return it to the dish and add the chicken. Warm through for five minutes and serve with roast potatoes and green beans.

Suggested beer accompaniment

Obviously cider or perry would be a good accompaniment, but a decent geueze, or even a wheat beer (Tesco's French wheat beer is fabulous), would go equally well.

Belgian Chowder

For this recipe, I have taken the New England thick potato soup, clam chowder, and adapted it to arrange a marriage between Belgian Geuze (pronounced 'hurser') which I feel is one of my most successful meals. With a healthy input of potatoes and a full consistency, I can quite happily say that the 'soup' is definitely a meal on its own. The recipe serves six.

Ingredients

3 tablespoons vegetable oil
1 medium onion, chopped
3oz white flour, sieved
3/4 pint milk
3/4 pint fish stock
1 can Baxter's Lobster Bisque
½ litre Gueze (or 1 glass white wine) – as an alternative use ½ litre La Choffe plus 1 glass white wine mixed together
3-4 bayleaves
Pinch salt
Large teaspoon ground black pepper
4-5 medium potatoes

Method

1. De-gas the gueze by pouring from glass to glass and place to one side. Note Sainsbury's Gueze or Frank Boon Gueze are particularly suitable. Don't use a very sour gueze.

2. Peel and dice potatoes into 1 inch cubes; par boil until just undercooked (about 8 minutes) and place on one side.

3. Heat oil in a large saucepan (at least 4 pints), lightly fry the onion with the bayleaves. Don't allow the onion to brown.

4. Add flour and stir well to form an even, creamy roux. Again, don't allow to brown.

5. Add pepper and then slowly combine half the milk, stirring in a figure of eight to keep the texture smooth.

6. Add the lobster bisque and stir in.

7. Increase the heat, stirring all the time, and add the fish stock.

8. Turn the heat back down and slowly add the gueze.

9. Add the potatoes and stir in.

10. Adjust the thickness using the remaining milk.

You now have a basic chowder. However, the dish will be greatly enhanced by the addition of some kind of fish – crab, scampi, cod, haddock or even the dreaded clam (I find the shell fish rubbery and, in my opinion, it clashes with the other textures in the dish). My preferred option, however, is 4oz of prawns and two fillets of white haddock. Cut the haddock into bite-sized chunks and add these and the prawns to the chowder. Simmer for no more than 3 minutes, whether or not you add the fish.

Serving suggestion

Serve in soup bowls with a decent bread and enjoy.

Suggested beer accompaniment

Perhaps serve with an extra bottle (or three!) of gueze to wash it down.

Fruit Romanoff

Ingredients – for 4 people

1 punnet dark plums
6oz raspberries
2 lbs grapes
1 pint double cream
1 x 25cl bottle Duchesse du Bourgoigne
2-3 tablespoons caster sugar
1 glass Port
a little lemon juice

Method

Halve and de-stone the plums and place in a large mixing bowl together with the grapes and raspberries. Squirt 4 to 5 drops of lemon juice over the fruit. Pour in the port and mix well. Then open the beer and leave for one hour during which time you should place the bowl of fruit in a refrigerator. After 50 minutes start whipping the cream with a hand whisk, noting that whisking should be continuous. The cream should be able to stand in stiff peaks when the whisk is withdrawn. Take half the cream and using a large spoon gently combine it with the fruit, at the same time, and bit by bit, adding the beer. Place this mixture in a serving dish and gently smooth the rest of the cream on top.

Serving suggestion

Some of the grapes and raspberries could be saved for decoration and, as a final embellishment, a little of the cream could be mixed with red food colouring and topped on to the tips of the cream.

Suggested beer accompaniment

Serve with Zywicc porter or Ceres stout – believe me it works!

Eastern Poussin in Artois Bock

To some, the combination of Tandoori style chicken, (small chickens – poussin, in this case), with Belgium beer may seem an exotic, nay, esoteric flight of madness! Yet ponder ye well. Beer drinkers of the British ilk favour in great numbers the cuisine of the sub-continent, so my idea ain't so bad after all:- try it, I think you'll be quite pleased with the experience.

Ingredients (For Two People)

2 poussin (or spatchcock)
1 450gm tub of yoghurt
3 tablespoons mild paprika
1 tablespoon tumeric
½ cup methi leaves
2 small chillies – crushed and chopped
3 large cloves of garlic
2 teaspoons ginger powder or chopped fresh ginger
¼ pint Artois Bock (available at Tesco or Morrisons)
½ teaspoon black pepper
1 teaspoon salt
6 drops lemon juice
2 teaspoons tomato puree   (A little milk)?

Method

Split the poussin in two down to the breast bone and lay in a casserole dish or roasting dish. De-gas the beer and stand for at least ½ hour, (an hour is better).

Combine all other ingredients in mixing bowl. Add the beer, and ensure that an even, smooth, thin paste is achieved. If it appears too thick, thin down with a little milk.

Make a small ½ inch deep cut in each thigh, and on each breast of the poussin, and coat evenly with the tandoori paste.

Cook in the middle of a 200 degree oven for 20-25 mins; after which, move to a higher shelf and turn the temperature to 450 degrees, brown for 5-6 mins, then turn over and repeat.

Serving suggestion

Serve with basmati rice, or mushroom risotto as shown elsewhere.

Suggested beer accompaniment

Drink with the Artois Bock or a chilled wheat beer, or perhaps a crisp medium dry perry.

Belgian beers, with their subtle variations in flavour, are particularly useful in cooking .

Winter

Irish Stew (guest recipe)

Ingredients

2k of diced lamb, marinated for 2 hours in Rosemary and 1 pint Guiness
1 onion
1k carrots
8-9 new potatoes

Method

Fry onion in large pan, once onion is soft add your lamb. Wait for the lamb to cook thoroughly, add half bottle of red wine and your rosemary and Guiness. Leave for ten minutes whilst the juices come to the boil.

Chop down your carrots finely, leave carrots to go soft usually around ½ hour.

Then you simply add your new potatoes and just wait until they are good and soft. Then serve.

By Thomas Greenhalgh
The Knot Fringe
Deansgate

Barnsley Chops in Stout Sauce

Ingredients

4 Double Lamb Chops (i.e. not split at the spine) or 8 Leg chops
2 medium onions
4oz flour   A little oil
2 tablespoons tomato puree
1½ pints sweet stout or porter
2 beef stock cubes
Salt, pepper and a pinch of mustard powder

=Method

Place the chops in a roasting tin and brush with oil. Cook in a medium oven for 30 minutes.

Meanwhile, prepare the sauce, thus:

Heat a little oil in a 2 or 3 pint saucepan.

Chop and finely dice the onions and gently fry in the oil until soft. Slowly add the flour to make a roux.

Dissolve the stock cubes in a little boiling water, and slowly blend in. together with the seasoning.

Stir in the tomato puree (be careful to make sure the roux is not too dry – cut down on the flour if necessary).

Stir rapidly until the roux browns.

De-gas the stout/porter if it is bottled by passing between two vessels until the head subsides.

Slowly and gradually add the stout/porter to the roux. It is advisable to check the heat or occasionally remove the pan from the heat, in order to keep the sauce lump free.

Slowly simmer for 10 minutes stirring all the time. Add some water if the sauce becomes too thick.

Coat the chops in the sauce and serve with boiled potatoes and green beans, or whatever you fancy!

Brown Ale Goulash

Ingredients (for 4 people)

2 large pork fillets
1 x 12oz can chopped tomatoes
2-3 teaspoons hot paprika (use 1½ teaspoons of Cayenne pepper instead)
3 finely chopped cloves of garlic
20 small potatoes (or buy the ready peeled packs)
2 small onions, finely chopped
4oz flour
½ pint Brown Ale – Thwaites Brown is ideal
1 pint stock
2 tablespoons olive oil
20 pieces bought Gnocchi (fresh)

Method

Gently sweat the onions in the olive oil for 4 minutes, meanwhile dice the pork into 1" cubes, then add to the pan and seal for two minutes each side. Finely sift in the flour and colour until light brown, then add a little of the beer until a stiff paste is formed. Add the garlic and paprika stir in – then add the tomatoes. Slowly combine the rest of the liquid until a thin sauce is obtained.

Cook the gnocchi and potatoes in a separate pan by boiling for 8 minutes, drain and put to one side.

You now have two choices – you can either serve the dish with everything in, or serve the gnocchi and potatoes separately. If electing the first way, then add the gnocchi to the pork/sauce and simmer for 6 minutes, then add the potatoes and simmer for a further 3 minutes. For the second way simply simmer the gnocchi and potatoes separately for the same period, whilst simmering the main dish for 9 minutes.

Garnish with soured cream and a little dry paprika, and I particularly enjoy fresh green beans with this meal, or, if there are any left from Christmas, try some sprouts.

Spicy Lancashire Beer Ragout

Ingredients (for 4 people)

4 horseshoe or 2 straight plain white puddings
4 horseshoe or 2 straight black puddings
8 pork sausages
3 lbs sage and onion stuffing
12oz tin chopped tomatoes
2 tsp ground ginger
½ tsp cayenne pepper
1 tsp ground black pepper
½ pint porter
1 pint vegetable stock
1 tbs vegetable oil   *1 Medium Onion (chopped)*
1 bayleaf (large)   *salt*
(NB Black/White Puddings come in many types, allow 4oz per person)

Method

Heat the oil in a large saucepan and gently fry the onion. Meanwhile make up a warm stock. Add 2/3rds of the stuffing to the saucepan, combine and remove from the heat. Cut puddings into ½ inch thick rounds, the sausages in half, and grill, for 5 minutes each side. Mix half the stock with the remaining stuffing and set to one side.

Add the sausages and puddings to the saucepan with the stuffing and onion. Return to the heat and add the tomatoes, when bubbling, slowly add the porter until a thick sauce results. Add the unused stock to thin down, then the remaining ingredients (except the stock/stuffing mixture previously set aside) and simmer for five minutes. Top the mixture (thinned down with worcester sauce and water if required) with the stock and stuffing mix and bake in a hot oven on the top shelf until lightly browned (7 or so minutes).

Suggested beer accompaniment

Wash down with a local standard bitter.

Ram Tam – Yam Yam

The vegetable dish can be used as a main meal or as a side dish for roasts, grills, curries or my own favourite – breast of tandoori chicken.

Ingredients

4-6 sweet potatoes (see note at end)
1 medium cauliflower
1 medium tin of white or red kidney beans
2 onions
2 tablespoons paprika
3 cloves of garlic, finely diced
2 teaspoons tomato puree
2 teaspoons ground ginger (or minced fresh ginger)
½ teaspoon salt
½ teaspoon chilli powder
1 pint Taylor's Ram Tam (or any sweet stout or porter)
2 pints of water (approx.)
Cooking oil

When purchasing many of these ingredients, a good class Indian or Asian store is both economical and offers better quality ingredients, although all of the above items can be obtained from the larger national supermarket chains. When buying sweet potatoes, try picking the longer, thinner ones – and look for a slight purplish tinge to the skin. Discard any which appear soft.

Method

1. Peel sweet potatoes and cut into ½ inch slices. Then make sure each slice is about the size of a 50p coin – this could involve cutting some in half or even quartering.

2. Break the cauliflower into florets about the size of your thumb above the final joint.

3. Roughly dice the onions.

4. Gently heat the oil and fry the onions until just browning.

5. Add the cauliflower and fry for 2 minutes, stirring constantly.

6. Add sweet potatoes and fry for a further 2 minutes, stirring constantly.

7. Add the remaining solid ingredients, stirring in well.

8. Add water and bring to the boil. Boil *very* vigorously until reduced by half and then turn down to a simmer. The liquid needed can vary considerably according to utensils and the type of cooking appliance used. Therefore, only add half the water to begin with – repeat if mixture is too thick, or add more than the 2 pints if too thin, but only after adding the beer.

9. Add all the beer and gradually increase the heat until boiling. Boil vigorously for 2 minutes, stirring constantly.

10. Test the sweet potatoes and cauliflower – if underdone again boil vigorously (you may need to add more water). Serve when they are reasonably soft.

Serving suggestion

The dish is now ready to serve. However, the appearance will be greatly enhanced by a further process. Peel and thinly slice two more sweet potatoes (rounder ones are better for this), gently fry for 30 seconds each side or brush with oil and grill for the same period. Place the slices over the cooked dish to give a mouth-watering finish.

Suggested beer accompaniment

Medium dry cider, gueze or a Belgian peach beer might well be your choice to accompany this meal. Cheers!

Real Ale Pie

The basic recipe can be altered to suit individual needs. If small individual pies are your choice, then use short crust pastry. Because of the extra pastry, the filling should be enough for 8-10 portions. If, however, a larger, single pie is to be cooked, then for ease use puff pastry. Depending on the cook's generosity, 6-8 portions can be expected. The choice of ales is personal, based on the experience I have gained through cooking this dish over a two-year period, at least once a week. The two ale method gives best results, however it is more time-consuming, and using only Old Peculier the result is still highly rich and satisfying.

Ingredients

3 lb braising steak
3 lamb's kidneys or 1 pig's kidney (optional)
2 medium onions, finely chopped
2 oz flour
1 ½ pints Theakston Old Peculier or 1 pint Taylor's Landlord and ½ pint Old Peculier
3 tablespoons mild paprika
6 cloves
2 teaspoons tomato puree
6 medium or 4 large bayleaves
2 teaspoons ground black pepper
2 cloves garlic
1 dessert spoon salt
6-10 dashes Worcestershire Sauce (optional)
1 cup gravy made with one dessert spoon granules or powder (Oxo original works well)
Short crust or puff pastry (home-made or frozen)

Method

1. Dice and trim the braising steak into 1-inch cubes. If using kidney, cut into ¼ inch pieces (and be sure to remove the white core).

2. Peel and slice the garlic; spread the salt on a chopping board and chop the garlic in the salt; finally, crush the chopped garlic into the salt using the base of a knife.

3. If using the two-beer method, transfer rapidly between two vessels to de-gas it. Then place the meat in the beer and leave for 10 minutes (if you are making your own pastry, this could be a good time to do so).

4. Take a large pan (preferably a flame proof casserole) and gently heat enough oil to cover the bottom to a depth of 1/8 inch; add the onions and fry gently until golden.

5. Drain the meat from the ale (keeping the beer for later) then, increasing the heat, add the meat to the pan and fry, stirring all the time, until the meat is sealed. About 2-3 minutes.

6. Stir in the paprika, black pepper, cloves and bay leaf.

7. Add the flour, stirring continuously, until the meat is covered and keep frying until the flour is brown

8. Mix in the tomato puree, garlic and Worcestershire sauce.

9. Add   made-up gravy and stir well in.

10. Then gradually add one pint of ale until a sauce the consistency of single cream is achieved. Dilute with water if it is too thick.

11. Simmer until just bubbling, stirring all the time.

12. If using a flame proof casserole this can then be placed straight in the oven, otherwise transfer the mixture to a pre-heated oven dish. Cook at gas mark 5, 175F for 2½ hours, stirring every 45 minutes, adding a little of the remaining ½ pint of ale each time.

13. Roll out the pastry. If making individual pies, line the pie dishes and bake blind for 10-12 minutes at gas 7, 425F. Then leave to cool for 20 minutes. Then fill with meat and sauce, cover with pastry cap, brush with egg wash (that's one egg whisked with a little milk) and return to oven for a further 15 minutes or until golden.

14. If making a larger pie, add the filling to the pie dish, cover with pastry top and bake at gas 7, 425F for 10 minutes. Remove from the oven, brush with egg wash and return to the oven for a further 7-10 minutes, or until golden.

Serving suggestions

Served with boiled potatoes and green beans.

Suggested beer accompaniment

A good best bitter makes an ideal accompaniment to this. Taylor's Landlord, Adnams Broadside or something similar can be recommended.

An Alternative Christmas Dinner

Here is a vegetarian alternative to roast turkey, etc., using different beers to impart a richness of flavour. Firstly there is a cheese and tomato soup, followed by a pulse and nut roast and to finish serve a traditional Christmas pudding. All recipes serve 4.

Cheese & Tomato Soup

6 beef tomatoes
1 medium onion
4 oz flour
4 oz grated cheese
1 bottle (½ pint) pale ale or Hapkin Belgian Ale

Method

1. Place grated cheese in a bowl and pour the beer over. Leave to soak.

2. Slit the tomatoes at the head and place in boiling water for 1 minute. Cool and remove the skins.

3. Heat a little oil in a 2-3 pint saucepan. Finely chop the onion and sweat until golden.

4. Stir in the flour to make a roux and stir in until going brown. Gradually blend in the cheese/beer mix until all has been absorbed.

5. Finally, make up to 1 pint using water, milk, or water and cream as desired, until a thick creamy consistency is achieved.

6. Remove the core and pips from the tomatoes and roughly chop the flesh. Add to the sauce, stirring well in.

7. Adjust the seasoning and then thin to a soup consistency using water. Heat to just below boiling and simmer on a low light for 5 minutes.

Serving suggestions

Serve with croutons.

Pulse and Nut Roast with Beer Gravy

Ingredients

8oz dried red lentils
8oz dried black eye beans
8oz crushed mixed nuts
4 cloves garlic
teaspoon chilli powder
teaspoon fenugreek
1 pint porter or stout
2 eggs
salt and pepper

8oz dried red kidney beans
410gm tin chick peas
4oz flour
2 medium onions

(You can of course use dried chick peas but they take far longer to cook than the other pulses. Red lentils on the other hand cook very quickly and should be cooked separately from the beans.)

Method

Soak the pulses overnight. Drain; boil rapidly for 10 minutes and the more gently until soft – about 45 minutes but test after 30. Drain well and place in a large mixing bowl with the drained chick peas. Roughly mash. Then blend in the eggs.

Finely chop the onions and garlic and blend in (you can soften them in a little oil first, if you wish).

Then add the nuts, chilli and fenugreek. Mix well using the hands and gradually add the flour until a stiff dough is formed. Add the stout or porter, using the hands to work it in. Form into a log shape, foil wrap and cook in a medium oven for 25 minutes.

Serving Suggestion – Beer Gravy

Make up a standard gravy mix, but lessen the water content, to achieve a very thick sauce. Thin down with pale ale or stout.

Mixed Game Pie

Ingredients

1 Hare (skinned and dressed)
1 Wood Pigeon (plucked)
1 male Pheasant (plucked)
1 wild duck (Mallard)
1 bottle Rochefort-8°
1 bottle Old Tom
½ bottle of Port
½ pint date vinegar or light Balsamic
2 tsp English mustard (wet)
2 tsp dried marjoram
2 large cloves of garlic
2 tbsp tomato puree
1 packet of frozen short-crust pastry
Salt and pepper to taste

Method

Divide the hare into natural joints (do not smoke!). That is, the legs into two, torso into four and forget the head.

Similarly, joint the birds into pieces about the same size as the hare pieces (not wings!).

In a vessel large enough to contain these comfortably, deposit the game and cover with boiling water.

Leave to stand for 1 hour. Do not go to the pub! Instead, mix half the Rochefort, half the Old Tom and all other fluids in a large mixing bowl.

Combine all other ingredients, except the pastry. Now you can go to the pub, but return within 1 hour.

Take the game from the water and painstakingly, laboriously finger-achingly remove the flesh from the bone (don't worry; after this you've earned another visit to the pub!). Place in the marinade – for so is the nomenclature used for the reddish liquid you made before – and go to the pub. Game can be left in the marinade for at least 24 hours, but 48 hours would be better. However, make sure it is kept refrigerated.

When ready, drain the game and place into a casserole or roasting dish.

Take the liquid and gently heat in a large pan. Then stir in a little instant gravy powder until quite stiff (no titters please). Let down with the beer you should have saved and pour into the pie dish/casserole.

Bake for 2 hours in a 200°F oven.

Roll out the pastry and cover the pie dish. Return to the oven for 15-20 minutes. Gradually increase the temperature to 300°F. Brush with egg wash and serve.

Suggested beer accompaniment

What do you drink with this? An old ale or Porter may seem well-suited and I would be happy to drink, say Sarah Hughes Mild or Lees Moonraker with this dish. But to keep things simple or weird, some would say, try a cocktail of Rochefort-8° and Old Tom. As a contrast, a blonde beer, Isle of Arran or Roosters Yankee for example, would appear to match nicely.

Why not serve a Fruit Romanoff (recipe page 48) for pud?

Guest Recipe

German Shepherd's Pie With Rot Kohl

Ingredients

First catch a German Shepherd and get him to sell you 1½ lbs of leg or loin lamb, then take these other ingredients:

1-2 tbsp vegetable oil
1 large or 2 medium onions
1 vegetable stock cube
1 tsp German mustard
½ pint of Erdinger Dunkel
A little gravy mix (vegetable, if possible)
1-1½ lbs mashed potatoes
Salt and pepper to taste

Method

Gently heat 1 tbsp of oil and fry the onions until golden brown.

Add the minced lamb and vegetable stock and stir until browned.

Mix the gravy with hot water to a stiff paste, then let down with a little Dunkel.

Reduce the heat and stir this in, being careful not to get sticky bits on your bottom (Not my words! – Ken.)

Slowly add the rest of the Dunkel and, very gently, simmer for 15-20 minutes.

Adjust the seasoning and top with mashed potatoes in an ovenproof dish. Brush with eggwash and brown under the grill.

Rot Kohl

Ingredients

2 lb red cabbage
1 large Bramley apple or 2 medium Granny Smith's
2-3 bay leaves
1-1½ glasses white wine
2 tsp honey
1-1½ tsp cider vinegar
¼ lb butter
Salt and pepper to taste

Method

Slice up the cabbage into 2 inch x ½ inch strips. Peel and slice the apples similarly.

Melt the butter and fry gently with seasoning and bay leaves. After 2 minutes of constant stirring, add the rest of the ingredients and blend together.

Serve immediately or refrigerate for future use.

A few slices of crusty bread would go well with this dish, as, of course, would another bottle, or two of Dunkel!

The liquid needed can vary considerably according to utensils and the type of cooking appliance used. Therefore only add half of the water to begin with. Repeat if the mixture is too thick, or add more than the 2 pints if too thin, but only after adding the beer.

Det
The Crescent, Salford

Cerises Rodenbach

As Yuletide approaches, I thought hard of several alternatives to the usual fare. Several game dishes involving rich stouts, old ales or hefty abbey beers make a seasonally appropriate choice. I almost plumped for Christmas pudding, which any cook worth their salt would literally soak with Guinness. However, I have decided to offer a simpler and lighter sweet, to complement your traditional Christmas bird. The dish is easy to make yet is, I think, a very satisfying end to any meal, but especially the gut-bustin' turkey dinner that many of us get stuffed with.

Ingredients (serves 4)

2 tins of black or red cherries or 1lb of stoned fresh cherries   *4 oz caster sugar*
1 pint fresh double cream   *1 350 cl bottle of Rodenbach*
2 double measures (10 cl) of port

Method

1. Empty the cherries into a bowl, and drain off all the preserving syrup.

2. Open the Rodenbach and de-gas: use a vessel at least twice the size of the bottle (you'll need two such vessels), and pour carefully, between the vessels, until most of the froth has subsided.

3. Pour onto the cherries and leave to soak, preferably overnight, but for at least two hours.

4. Whip the cream until it is stiff enough to stand in soft peaks but be careful not to over whip (unless you're into S&M) – sorry!

5. Stir the sugar into the port until it has dissolved, then gently fold it into the cream until it becomes an even cherry hue.

6. Combine the cream with the Rodenbach soaked cherries until all are evenly covered, and then even out the sauce in the serving dish.

7. Chill in a refrigerator for at east 30 minutes.

The sweet is now ready to serve but the appearance will be enhanced by some form of decoration – sponge fingers, milk chocolate fingers, meringue shells or tinned fruit or use your own imagination to make a truly festive-looking dish. Just a couple of points. Rodenbach is usually on sale at The Beer House or Bar Eringe or can be obtained from M Kinderman. Good Eating. Good Drinking and Wassaill.

The Beers – Some Notes

Artois Bock

From the Leuven brewery in Belgium, more famous for its Stella brand, this fruity, aromatic amber beer is a better example of Belgiums unique beer styles. Wildely available in supermarkets such as Morrisons, Tesco and Sainsburys. 6.2% a.b.v.

Bazens – Black Pig Mild

Is a fine example of a not too sweet, dark mild, which can have flavours of coffee and chocolate. Only available in the north, so try to get a similar mild if you can't find this one. 3.6% a.b.v.

Bulmers No. 1

The classic dry, (some cider drinkers would say medium dry), bottled cider, gives a woody appley taste. There are, thankfully many other dry ciders available from supermarkets. These would do equally as well in cookery. 7.2% a.b.v.

Belgium Fruit Beers

A lambic (q.v.) beer to which fruit or fruit syrup has been added; this classically was local cherries which were fermented in a secondary process with the beer. Now, however, fruit syrup or concentrate is added. This is anathaema to the true avicionado, but makes little difference when used in cooking.

Flavours are Kriek (cherry), Framboise or Frambozen (raspberries), Peche (peach), and Cassis, (blackcurrant): banana, plum and pineapple beers should be restricted to moods of mirthful madness! The most common brands are Timmermans, Belle Vue, Liefmans and Lindemans.

Brown Ale

In Britain, a dark, commonly bottled, version of mild; although this has variants such as Newcastle Brown Ale or Nut Brown Ale:- using these variants would result in a slightly different flavour to the dish; to put it another way, you could produce your own bespoke version of the dish.

In Belgium, brown ale is a completely different species, sometimes known as oude or oude brune it tastes like no other beer – the nearest I can manage as a description is, like a gaelic or brandy coffee with blackberries added, and then watered down.

The extremely rare Liefmans Oude is the supreme classic example.

Budvar

The original Budweiser, from Budvice in the Czech Republic, this native pilsner should on no account be confused with the U.S. (or should that be u.s.), version – produced from the very cheapest fermentable grains, and for all I know, rat droppings, to end up with something wet and alcoholic. To call it a beer would insult brewers anywhere!

Geuze

A lambic q.v. beer from Belgium using a blend of matured and younger beers.

Giradin

A rare, lemony geuze, which may be hard to find. As a substitute any not too tart geuze may be used.

Duchesse De Bourgogne

A delicately winey, fruity Flemish ale, (top fermented), matured in oak casks, with flavours typical of French Flanders, (although brewed just over the Belgium border): it's the native yeasts of the area which give this great beer its apple and berry notes – a wonderful cooking, and sipping beer. 6.2% a.b.v.

Hapkin

A light, delicate ale, with a touch of lager flavour, produced near the hop growing region of Flanders. The low bitterness of these hops gives a slightly flowery nose to this beer. Very good to flavour or accompany any fish dish. 6.0% a.b.v.

Isle of Arran Blonde

Typical of a style of ale invented by West Coast U.S.A. micro-brewers – now increasingly popular with British brewers. Easy drinking, flowery hops with only a hint of bitterness are characteristic of these blond, yellow or American ales – as they are known. This is widely available in supermarkets – ask if not in stock. 5.0% a.b.v.

Kriek

See Belgium beers.

La Chouffe Blonde Speciale

Brewed in the Ardennes this fruity, exhuberant, limey, deceptively drinkable beer may remind you of a fizzy wine:- naturally it comes in 750cl Champagne style bottles. Available in supermarkets. 8.0% a.b.v.

Lambic

Is uniquely brewed using wild yeasts from the surrounding area. These are let into the brewery via windows, or slats in the window frames and are akin to wine yeasts. Lambics are aged for varying periods.

Liefmans Goudenband

Deceptively light on the palate, this winey, limey, scintillatingly sparkling nectar nevertheless packs a powerful punch: sip it or swill it, or sip, then swill, it can get one forgetfully merry with devilish ease.

In cooking be very watchful of the heat, as the subtle fruitiness can slip away wraithlike. 9.0% a.b.v.

J.W. Lees Moonraker

Heavy, dark and rich the full flavour gives a warming satisfaction. Robust enough to stand some mistakes in cooking.

Old Peculiar

Similar to the above, but less sweet, with a more hoppy aftertaste.

Old Tom

Again, a heavy old ale, it can seem slightly more alcoholic than the other two.

Peche

See Belgium fruit beers.

London porter – circa 1850 – probably tastes something like ₉hes Mild q.v. Now any dark, strongish, not too bitter ale can have this .ature. For cooking purposes any porter in a storm etc.

---

e Ale

ₐ widely used term which can be applied to countless different beers. Basically use a 4% to 5% beer, and with any ingredient, the better the quality, the better the dish will be.

Sierra Nevada Pale Ale

Is a lesson to some British brewers in what this proto-British ale should be like: Sierra Nevada is named after the mountain range in California. 5.0% a.b.v.

Rodenbach 80

Is a fine example of Belgium red beer, and is the lowest strength brewed; 10% and 12% versions are the others.

Rich in berry, coffee and molasses flavours, the suggestion of fortified red wine may be the strongest taste detected:- which makes it ideal for sweets. The thing to beware of is adding too much liquid, in an attempt to bring out all its flavours. Can be somewhat tart.

Roosters Yankee

Sean Franklins beers lean heavily towards stateside, (see blonde beers – Isle of Arran), this straw coloured, beautifully hopped ale, hammers the ball back over the Atlantic and says, "beat that"!

Sarah Hughes Mild

Has revived the strength of yesteryear, when foundry workers and their kind, would need an easy drinking, hydrating, yet satisfying quencher after work.

Discovered from an old recipe and brewed in the small brewhouse behind The Beacon Hotel, Sedgeley, in the Black Country, people nowadays usually treat this ale as they would a porter (q.v.)

Timothy Taylors' Landlord

Has won so many awards that the boardroom is running out of wall-space; however, they keep coming for this most perfect of Best Bitters. A fine mouthfeel and clean, slightly flowery nose, leads to expectation of a full drinking experience: an expectation realised in the final gulp, and the full finish and aftertaste. Heat with care, as the bitterness can result from too fierce a ring (gas or electric)! 4.3% a.b.v.

Timothy Taylors' Ram Tam

Is dark, but not black, with a beautiful blend of roast malt, yeast and styrian hops. A strong mild? – weak old ale? , a subtle porter? No Ram Tam is in a class of its' own: cook with respect! 4.3% a.b.v.

Some Specialist Beer Suppliers

Beer Direct — Stoke-on-Trent

Tel: 01782 303823

Belgium Beer Imports (UK) — Woking

Tel: 01483 740984

Beer Ritz — (Mail Order)

Tel: 01423 359371

Belgian Belly — Wilbraham Road, Chorlton, Manchester

Tel: 0161 860 6766

www.belgianbelly.com

Bottles — 349 Commercial Road, London E 1 2PS

Tel: 020 7265 8388

www.onlyfinebeer.co.uk

Cave Direct — Surrey

Tel: 020 8303 2261

www.belgiumbeersuk.com

James Clay — Elland, West Yorkshire

Tel: 01422 377560

Nectar Imports — Wilts

Tel: 01747 840100

www.nectar.net

Scottish Courage — 160 Dundee St. Edinburgh (Alken, Maes-Grimbergen)

Tel: 0131 6565000

Ken Birch seeking inspiration for another great recipe.

Printed in the United Kingdom
by Lightning Source UK Ltd.
110436UKS00001B/280-354